To:

From:

THE HEART OF CHRISTMAS

Susan Squellati Florence

The C.R. Gibson Company, Norwalk, CT 06856

December dawns,
the days are shorter,
the gold leaves
    have fallen
and a chill
    is in the air.

We light the lantern
    of Christmas
to seek its warm
    and loving heart.

We take time
to renew
the spirit of living,
to illuminate
what brings us meaning

and to prepare
for the birth
of love
in our hearts.

We hang wreaths of green
as a sign of welcome,
opening our homes
and hearts
to renewed life
and love.

For young
and old alike

the Christmas carols
bring music
to our souls.

Favorite family recipes
fill the home
with wonderful scents

and the promise
of festive times
we will share.

We take time
to remember
special people
who have touched
our lives ...

and we send them
wishes of love,
happiness
and good health.

We are all children
as we gaze
in wonder and delight
upon the glowing
Christmas tree.

Each ornament,
carefully placed,
shines in the light
of its own
special meaning.

We read again
and reflect again
upon the beautiful
and simple story
of the first Christmas.

We are reminded
that the love
brought to the world
by the Christ child
is needed now
in each of our hearts.

And the radiant
star of peace
that shone in the heavens
that night
needs to shine
even brighter.

The heart
of Christmas
holds for each of us
a special meaning.

For as much as Christmas
is many voices singing,
so too is Christmas
one silent prayer
for peace.

And as much as Christmas
is a wondrous
starry night,
so too is Christmas
one candle burning.

And as Christmas
is giving gifts,
it is also knowing the gifts
we already have ...
love,
beauty,
joy,
family,
friends,
life.

Christmas
is a time
to remember
special people
who touch
our lives.

and a time to offer
lovingkindness
to people
we do not know
whose lives
we can touch.

Christmas is a time
to share,
to celebrate,
to be with others
and a time
to be with yourself.

Look deep within
this heart of Christmas.

Know its love
and feel its light
entering your heart
and illuminating your life.